Rock My World Quiz Book

Dedicated to Larry and all the Rock
My Worlders

Copyright © 2020 Paul Rance

ISBN: 9798698612827
Imprint: Independently published

Cover and interior design by Paul Rance

Cover photograph and cartoon by Paul Rance

A Peace & Freedom Press book

Peace & Freedom Press online
http://www.pandf.booksmusicfilmstv.com/

Contents

610 Questions
Pages 9-69
Answers 71-82

Rock Mathematics
Page 84
Answers 89

Rock Alphabet
Pages 85-86
Answers 89

Rock Geography
Pages 87
Answers 89

Rock Biology
Pages 88
Answers 89, 90

Introduction

This is a book that I had the germ of an idea from my Rock My World Facebook group.

This is definitely not a book aimed at rock music nerds, as they will, no doubt, find the questions ridiculously easy. But, for the casual rock fan, I hope there's fun to be had maybe getting more correct answers than a self-confessed expert on all things rock.

Play nice.

- Paul Rance, October 2020.

With a pencil keep a record of your score

Your opponent's score

The Beatles

1. What was the name of the drummer Ringo Starr replaced?

2. Which year was George Harrison born?

3. What was the name of John Lennon's first wife?

4. Which Beatles track was the first to feature a sitar?

5. Which of these towns and cities did The Beatles never play? Luton, Bolton, Peterborough, Derby, Ayr, Newport, Belfast.

6. Which Beatle spent three years in hospital as a child?

7. Which Beatles album was originally going to be called 'Everest'?

8. Who designed the 'Sgt. Pepper' album cover?

9. Which film featured The Beatles playing on a rooftop?

10. Who played lead guitar on the George composition 'While My Guitar Gently Weeps'?

Rock Chicks

1. For Chrissie Hynde there's a thin line between what?

2. Kim Wilde sang about the kids from where?

3. Which Grace sang of a white rabbit?

4. Joan Jett's group had a heart of a certain colour?

5. Who was spellbound in a Hong Kong garden?

6. Who joined Fleetwood Mac at the same time as Lindsay Buckingham?

7. Velvet Underground's Teutonic singer?

8. 'So What' was an album by which colourful American singer?

9. She fronted Big Brother and the Holding Company?

10. Punk bass icon with The Adverts?

The Kinks

1. A UK number one single from 1966?

2. Types of heroes from 1973?

3. A seasonal almanac?

4. 1967 story of Terry and Julie?

5. A Kinks album with a mythical king's name?

6. A mister with a nice nature?

7. A concept album and a preservation society for what?

8. 'Dedicated Follower of Fashion' was released in what year?

9. The famous winged guitar used by Dave Davies first appeared on what US pop music show?

10. This street, for The Kinks, was what?

David Bowie

1. Which song was David Bowie's first UK number one single?

2. What was David Bowie's real name?

3. Which special guest was a backing singer on Bowie's first US number one, 'Fame'?

4. Which European city did Bowie and Iggy Pop live in in the '70s?

5. Which pop idol was Bowie's guitarist on his 'Glass Spider' tour?

6. The joint David Bowie and Queen number one, 'Under Pressure', came about after a chance meeting in which European country?

7. 'The Bewlay Brothers', a track on the 'Hunky Dory' album, was about whom?

8. How did David Bowie end up with apparently different colour eyes?

9. Who designed the 'Hunky Dory' album cover?

10. Which rock and roll legend shares a birthday with David Bowie?

Love

1. 10cc tried to deny it in 1975, by saying?

2. T. Rex liked their love what?

3. Bowie was not stuck in the past with his type of love

4. Led Zeppelin song that became a theme tune on 'Top of the Pops'?

5. Jefferson Airplane sang that we needed '..... to Love'?

6. For The Troggs Love was what in 1967?

7. For Queen, love was what?

8. The Who wanted love to do what in 1973?

9. Lulu expressed her love to whom in this global smash hit of '67?

10. For The Sweet love was like what?

Punk/New Wave

1. Which band sang about a white riot?

2. An odd place for The Jam in 1979?

3. Which Howard was 'Shot By Both Sides'?

4. Was The Sex Pistols infamous Bill Grundy interview on the BBC or ITV?

5. What sort of bop did The Ramones sing about?

6. TV presenter and Factory Records boss?

7. Rodent Damned drummer?

8. Who sang about a girl who had lost control - again?

9. Who were 'So Lonely'?

10. Who didn't want to go to Chelsea?

Pink Floyd

1. Which girl did Pink Floyd see play in 1967?

2. The Floyd played at which out of this world venue in the '60s?

3. Who was told to be careful with that axe?

4. Which Roman ruins became a Floyd venue in the early '70s?

5. The three animals on the 'Animals' album?

6. 'Eclipse' ended which Pink Floyd album?

7. He howled on 'Meddle'?

8. What animal was featured on the 'Atom Heart Mother' cover?

9. Which song on the Floyd album 'The Wall' referred to a famous singer of the WWII years?

10. Pink Floyd's final album?

The Beach Boys

1. 'Good Vibrations' was released in which year?

2. Who sang the lead vocal on 'God Only Knows'?

3. True or false? Glen Campbell was once a member of The Beach Boys?

4. What was the name of The Beach Boys first single?

5. Which member of The Beach Boys visited India with The Beatles?

6. What animals featured on the 'Pet Sounds' cover?

7. Which girl did the group ask for help?

8. Who was the youngest member of The Beach Boys?

9. In 2013 The Beach Boys received their first ever Grammy award for which album?

10. True or false? Drummer Dennis Wilson never sang lead vocals on a Beach Boys song?

Places

1. The Beatles sang about thousands of holes in which English town?

2. Who sang about 'Oxford Town' on his 'Outside' album?

3. Neil Young's powerful song about the killing of students in 1970?

4. Where The Eagles notorious hotel was situated?

5. Simple Minds sang about a child from which Irish city?

6. Sex Pistols song about a great American city?

7. Sweet home was where for Lynyrd Skynyrd?

8. An English city where The Who's 1970 album was recorded?

9. Ultravox's song about a European capital?

10. A city that brought Coldplay's 'A Rush of Blood to the Head' album to a close?

Colours

1. Coldplay's 2000 hit?
2. New Order's type of Monday?
3. U2's '80s album was under what type of sky?
4. Prince song about which type of rain?
5. Visage faded to which colour?
6. Led Zeppelin's type of dog?
7. Colour of the Lemon Pipers tambourine?
8. Spandau Ballet were going for it?
9. Cream's room?
10. The Stones liked which type of sugar/girl?

Animals

1. They were wild and Susan Boyle covered this Stones song?

2. The type of days Florence Welch sang about?

3. This Byrds cetacean seemed happy?

4. The Beatles dug this animal on their 'Let It Be' album?

5. Survivor had the eye of this animal in the '80s?

6. Jefferson Airplane's white critter from 'Alice in Wonderland'?

7. Squeeze were cool for?

8. Meatloaf moved as fast as this creature?

9. This animal was on the run for Sweet in the '70s?

10. The Monkees song for a watery friend?

Radiohead

1. The first track on 'OK Computer'?

2. 'Creep' was a cover of a song by which group?

3. Which Radiohead album was first exclusively available over the Internet?

4. What year was 'Street Spirit (Fade Out)' released as a single?

5. The name of Thom Yorke's first solo album?

6. True or false? Radiohead were once the support act for Madonna?

7. The year the group was formed?

8. What inspired the group's name?

9 How many UK singles were released from the 'Amnesiac' album?

10. A numbers only single in 2003?

Psychedelic

1. Pink Floyd's Arnold - he had a strange hobby?

2. The Byrds were how many miles high in 1966?

3. A strange pillow for Jefferson Airplane?

4. Jimi Hendrix was 'All Along the Watchtower' in '68, but who wrote it?

5. What were the Beatles trying to fix on their 'Sgt. Pepper' album?

6. Iron Butterfly's 17 minute epic?

7. Group that included Andy Summers and Zoot Money?

8. Which band could see a long way in '67?

9. My beautiful friend was told what by The Doors?

10. The Small Faces sang about this idyllic park?

The Rolling Stones

1. Who replaced Brian Jones in The Stones?

2. What is Mick Jagger's middle name?

3. The Stones got their name from which famous bluesman?

4. Which Beatle appeared in 'Rock 'n' Roll Circus'?

5. What year was The Stones Hyde Park gig?

6. Did guitarist Ronnie Wood join The Stones in the 1970s or 1980s?

7. The Stones sang a song about 'Route __'?

8. Which famous cook created the cake, which appeared on the cover of the album, 'Sticky Fingers'?

9. This legendary songwriting duo penned The Stones first hit, 'I Wanna Be Your Man'?

10. Which famous political family were mentioned in the song, 'Sympathy for the Devil'?

Singers

1. Rod Stewart sang in which band with Julie Driscoll?

2. Robert Plant has sang with two groups that have the same name. What is the name?

3. What was Elvis Presley's middle name?

4. What is Elvis Costello's real name?

5. Which singer with a Factory Records band died months before John Lennon in 1980?

6. Who was called the Lizard King?

7. Who sang about a girl who wasn't all that she appeared to be in 1970?

8. Which member of The Police had been a schoolteacher?

9. Michael Hutchence reputedly had an affair with which British TV presenter?

10. Which punk legend sang on Leftfield's 'Open Up'?

Bassists

1. He felt Free with this legendary '60s trio?

2. Mr. Sumner from Newcastle, part of another legendary trio, but in the late '70s and early '80s?

3. This Bill went solo and a bit French in the '80s?

4. Andy starred with this precocious quartet, which also had Simon Kirke on drums?

5. Sid Vicious replaced him in The Pistols?

6. More than just another brick in the wall?

7. She canned it in the '70s?

8. He played with Hermans Hermits and then with Robert, Jimmy and John?

9. Pictured smashing his bass on 'London Calling'?

10. Red hot bassist who took his name from a small insect?

Drummers

1. Which experimental band, headed by a former punk singer, did Ginger Baker drum for in the '80s?

2. Former Beatle Ringo Starr's real name?

3. Female drummer for The Velvet Underground?

4. Heavy rock drumming legend who had a hit in the '70s with 'Dance with the Devil'?

5. Drummer for The Move and ELO?

6. Surname of John and Jason, who drummed for this famous combo?

7. He replaced Kevin Godley in 10cc?

8. Jim Morrison, Ray Manzarek, Robbie Krieger, and?

9. Plays guitar and sings, but originally just drummed for these grunge legends from Seattle?

10. Punk star, who drummed on Edwyn Collins 'A Girl Like You'?

Guitarists

1. Carlos, who sang of a 'Black Magic Woman'?
2. Damned but with a rank?
3. The tragic Rolling Stone, who died in '69?
4. Roger but also Jim?
5. Muse about him?
6. One name guitar hero, with a band Axl headed?
7. Big Country star who died young?
8. A spider and Bowie's right hand man for a time?
9. Doors axeman?
10. Just him and Meg became stars in an unusual duo?

Keyboardists

1. Elton John's real name?

2. Billy Preston played on which Beatles single?

3. Keith Emerson recorded 'America' with which '60s group?

4. Arguably the star turn on 'The Dark Side of the Moon'?

5. He famously played bass on his keyboards with The Doors?

6. Flamboyant keyboardist who appeared on Bowie's 'Hunky Dory'?

7. The one non-Joy Division member who was one of the original members of New Order?

8. LR who played at The Concert for Bangladesh?

9. Squeeze man who became a famous TV presenter?

10. Iain ------- Stones auxiliary member?

Neil Young

1. Neil was Rockin' where in 1986?

2. A film and Neil song?

3. A Crosby, Stills, Nash and Young song written by Neil about the Kent State massacre?

4. A 1976 2 disc collection of Neil's work?

5. The song which featured a mention of Johnny Rotten?

6. Neil used to have a peculiar mode of transport, when he drove a what?

7. Neil's backing band?

8. Seminal 1971 album?

9. Damning song on a Spanish conquistador?

10. He has been called the Godfather of what?

Numbers

1. The year where Zager and Evans pondered if Man would still be alive?

2. Closed U2's 'War' album?

3. The Proclaimers would walk this distance?

4. Noah and the Whale were thinking about how many years in the future?

5. Bryan Adams' Summer of?

6. The Stones were how many light years away from home in '67?

7. For The Beatles she was just?

8. Tears of And The Mysterians?

9. Arctic Monkeys Orwellian year?

10. Tom Robinson's motorway?

Jimi Hendrix

1. Jimi's middle name?

2. Which Animals bassist was Jimi's manager?

3. 'Ladyland' was what?

4. Earlier in his career, did Hendrix back Little Richard or Jerry Lee Lewis?

5. Did Jimi burn his guitar at the Monterey or Isle of Wight festival?

6. Hendrix's home town?

7. True or false? Jimi served in the Vietnam War?

8. Hendrix's group after The Jimi Hendrix Experience?

9. 'Kissing the Sky' hit?

10. Jimi Hendrix was part Cherokee or Sioux?

Heavy Rock

1. A quiet song from Uriah Heep in 1968?

2. This group were named after a medieval torture device?!

3. What was on the water for Deep Purple in 1972?

4. Which famous heavy metal guitarist lost fingers in an accident?

5. Ritchie Blackmore's colourful band?

6. The year that Judas Priest were founded?

7. Original name of Girlschool?

8. An Anglo-?

9. Lemmy of Motörhead's real name?

10. David Coverdale founded this group in the 1970s?

The Sex Pistols

1. Legendary early Pistols gig, 'The Screen On The -----'?

2. A barbed song about a certain record company?

3. Johnny Rotten used to wear a T-shirt professing to hate which group?

4. What TV show saw The Pistols first musical performance?

5. The name of Malcolm McLaren's shop which Paul Cook and Steve Jones worked in?

6. Who said his early equipment was stolen?

7. The real name of Sid Vicious?

8. A Sid cover of an Eddie Cochran song that made the UK singles chart in 1979?

9. Which year were the band formed?

10. Where was the group's last-ever live performance with Sid Vicious in the band?

Sun and Moon

1. Pink Floyd '60s potentially hot space journey?

2. Beatle George Harrison's optimistic song from '69?

3. Untypical Status Quo hit?

4. Sex Pistols last single, with Johnny Rotten as lead singer?

5. R.E.M. asked if you believed in this?

6. Creedence Clearwater Revival's ominous moon?

7. The Walker Brothers pessimistic song from '66?

8. For A-Ha, in '85, 'The Sun Always Shines on' what?

9. Manchester City fans adopted this '61 Marcells song?

10. Echo & The Bunnymen's deadly moon?

Bob Dylan

1. The title of Bob Dylan's debut album?

2. Bob Dylan's real name?

3. What album did 'Joey' appear on?

4. Which Dylan song gave The Byrds their first number one?

5. The film that covered Dylan's troubled tour of England in 1966?

6. The first song Dylan performed after he went electric?

7. When was 'Highway 61 Revisited' released?

8. What Beatles song did Dylan misinterpret as referring to drugs?

9. Which spaced out rock star recorded a tribute song to Dylan in 1971?

10. Which former Beatle recorded 'If Not For You'?

U2

1. What year was 'The Joshua Tree' released?

2. Who introduced U2 at Live Aid?

3. Which U2 song was about doomed INXS frontman Michael Hutchence?

4. What are Bono and The Edge's real names?

5. Early U2 album which was named after a month?

6. 'One' appeared on which U2 album?

7. What was unforgettable in 1984?

8. Which song did U2 and Paul McCartney perform together at Live 8 in 2005?

9. Who did a send-up of The Edge with Harry Enfield as Bono?

10. Which member of U2 was born in England?

Girls and Boys

1. An early Elvis Costello song?

2. He left for Spain on this '70s Elton hit?

3. Damned cover of a Paul Ryan classic?

4. A song sang by both Amy and The Zutons?

5. House of Love song/Stephen King novel?

6. Beatles dodgy Doctor?

7. Girl from an early U2 album?

8. Jilted John's moronic nemesis?

9. T-Rex's girl who looked like a zebra, or zeb-oh-ra?

10. The wind cried for Hendrix's girl?

The Byrds

1. Ballad of?

2. They just wanted to be friends with?

3. A song about a man and his simple musical instrument?

4. Mr. Riley?

5. A chestnut?

6. An album about those 'Notorious ---- Brothers'?

7. A song imploring us to move in the same way?

8. Jesus was just what?

9. More than the third dimension?

10. It was something she didn't care about?

Fleetwood Mac

1. Guitarist Jeremy Spencer was born in which North East town in England?

2. In what year was 'Albatross' released?

3. Which member of Fleetwood Mac wrote 'Songbird'?

4. Which iconic blues group did Peter Green, John McVie and Mick Fleetwood play in, pre-Fleetwood Mac?

5. What was the name of the Fleetwood Mac album that followed 'Rumours'?

6. Stevie Nicks and Lindsey Buckingham joined Fleetwood Mac in what year?

7. Peter Green and Mick Fleetwood were the original members of Fleetwood Mac. Who were the others?

8. What album did 'Rhiannon' appear on?

9. Apart from Peter Green, who was the other guitarist on 'Oh Well, Part 1'?

10. Which Fleetwood Mac song, written by Peter Green, supposedly summed up his personal strife?

Bruce Springsteen

1. Which New York punk poet and singer recorded 'Because the Night'?

2. The name of Bruce's revered band?

3. In which year was the 'Born to Run' single released?

4. Which group did Bruce appear with at the 2009 Glastonbury Festival?

5. For which film did Bruce win an Oscar for best song?

6. Which descendant of a famous '60s group recorded 'Blinded by the Light'

7. Early in his career Bruce was often compared to which legendary singer/songwriter?

8. 'My Hometown' appeared on which album?

9. The year of Bruce's debut album?

10. A summery song released in 2008?

Eric Clapton

1. The 'Beano' album featured Eric Clapton with which group?

2. The phrase in the '60s that deified Clapton?

3. Eric's birthdate?

4. Derek and the Dominos most well-known song?

5. What year did Eric leave The Yardbirds?

6. A short-lived group, which included Eric and Stevie Winwood?

7. Cream's last concert was where?

8. Who wrote Eric's hit 'I Shot the Sheriff'?

9. A 1977 song written about Pattie Boyd?

10. Who wrote 'Badge' with Eric Clapton?

The Moody Blues

1. The Moodies sang about this guru called Timothy -----?

2. The only UK number one single for The Moody Blues?

3. The first Moody Blues album to feature Justin Hayward?

4. He provided the band's poetry?

5. The Moody Blues were founded in which city?

6. What year was the group formed?

7. What were The Moodies searching for on their 1968 album?

8. Who sang the lead vocal on 'Go Now'?

9. Which member of The Moody Blues played the Mellotron?

10. 'Question' appeared on which Moody Blues album?

Days and Nights

1. Moody Blues '67 classic?
2. A bit of both for The Beatles in '64?
3. One word Kinks hit of '68?
4. Roy Orbison's long drive?
5. Rod Stewart '70s hit?
6. Poignant, reminiscing Queen song?
7. Moby Grape's joyful song?
8. John Lennon said it was alright in '74?
9. Stereophonics wished us well in 2001?
10. Daring Stones song of '67 and a Bowie cover?

Queen

1. 'Killer Queen' was a big UK hit single in what year?

2. Freddie Mercury's swipe at the record industry on 'A Night at the Opera'?

3. The video for which 1984 song saw Queen dressed in drag?

4. 'Radio Ga Ga' was allegedly inspired by?

5. Cheerful forerunner of Queen?

6. The single that followed 'Bohemian Rhapsody'?

7. Queen album title that shared its name with a now defunct British newspaper?

8. Queen's first US number one single?

9. Queen wrote the soundtrack for which 1980 sci-fi film?

10. The filmed 1986 Queen concert in Eastern Europe took place in which city?

Elton John

1. Elton's Captain was what?

2. His first UK hit?

3. Elton's first UK number one was the duet 'Don't Go Breaking My Heart' with Kiki Dee, but in what year?

4. Which T. Rex song did Elton play (mime!) on on 'Top of the Pops'?

5. Elton said he was still what in the '80s?

6. The original 'Candle in the Wind' was about which legendary Hollywood actress?

7. 'I Guess That's Why They Call It the -----'?

8. Which song featured a take on Pat Boone's 'Speedy Gonzalez'?

9. Elton's favourite football/soccer team?

10. The British label Elton was on when he became a star?

Rod Stewart

1. Rod Stewart recorded a song with Python Lee Jackson. What was it called?

2. What was Rod's first UK number one single?

3. 'Sailing' featured on which 1975 album?

4. Which group, formed by a former Yardbirds guitarist, did Rod Stewart front in the '60s?

5. 'You're in My Heart (The Final Acclaim)' was released in which year?

6. Which Rod double A-side single controversially kept 'God Save the Queen' by The Sex Pistols off the top of the UK singles chart in 1977?

7. Rod was a footballer at which club?

8. Faces 'Cindy'?

9. A Tim Hardin song which Rod had a reason to?

10. A series of albums of traditional American standards Rod recorded in the 21st Century?

Coldplay

1. The name of Coldplay's first studio album?

2. Chris Martin was born in what year?

3. 'Yellow' was a hit in 1999 or 2000?

4. How many studio albums have Coldplay released?

5. Coldplay come from which English city?

6. Where was Coldplay's first gig?

7. In what year did Coldplay win their first Grammy?

8. Which album did the song 'A Whisper' come from?

9. 'Warning Sign' was featured on which cult TV series starring Sarah Michelle Gellar?

10. The name of a famous cartoon character and the title of a song on 'Mylo Xyloto'?

Weather

1. It was, for Neil Young, 'Like a ---------'?

2. Oasis were originally named after this groundbreaking Beatles song?

3. The Kinks had this type of pleasant afternoon in '66?

4. Travis wondered why they were always a victim of this in '99?

5. The Doors rode this one?

6. Rain of an odd colour for Peter Gabriel?

7. The Searchers asked this question in '65?

8. Donovan once tried to catch it?

9. Cream's love was very bright?

10. Seminal Dylan anti-war song that blew?

The Police

1. Which member of The Police was in Curved Air?

2. True or false? Sting was once a teacher?

3. 'Every Breath You Take' was a hit in which year?

4. Which song was The Police's first American number one single?

5. What was the name of the last studio album released by The Police?

6. Sting's real name?

7. A early hit for The Police, which had a girl's name in the title?

8. Who was the youngest member of The Police?

9. What character did Sting play in the 'Quadrophenia' movie?

10. The Police's first record label?

1960s

1. There was 'Something in the Air' for these guys in 1969?

2. Cream asked if there was anyone for?

3. Which Black Sabbath member played briefly with Jethro Tull?

4. Female drummer on The Honeycombs 1964 UK number one single 'Have I the Right'?

5. Hollies frontman?

6. What type of arcade did Roy Orbison sing about in 1969?

7. The Soft Machine came from which Kentish city?

8. This Peanut Butter band were more like a what?

9. A Deadhead is what?

10. They were hot and canned?

1970s

1. 10cc song about a stewardess?

2. For Buzzcocks what EP had a scratch?

3. Boston's 'More Than a Feeling' came out in 1975, 1976, or 1977?

4. Christine McVie song on Fleetwood Mac's 'Rumours' covered by Eva Cassidy?

5. T. Rex's guru was what?

6. Kraftwerk song about this girl's profession?

7. Sweet's blitz was in a what?

8. Sex Pistols Stooges cover of a song about having no enjoyment?

9. Peter Frampton may have eaten it, but he was also in a band with this name?

10. What did Slade urge you to feel?

1980S

1. Phil Collins thought it was against all what in '84?

2. Dexy's hurry up call to a certain female?

3. Which famous British actress appeared in Adam Ant's 'Prince Charming' video?

4. Two times for Cyndi Lauper?

5. For Boy George war was what?

6. The Smiths pro-veggie hymn

7. OMD's two tributes to a French heroine?

8. Chrissie Hynde and UB40 topped the UK singles chart with a cover of this Sonny & Cher classic?

9. Foreigner wanted to know what in 1983?

10. Blondie's early take on rap appeared on which song?

1990s

1. R.E.M. were trying to push an elephant up the stairs in which 1999 song?

2. Oasis pondered about immortality in this song?

3. Stereophonics were just?

4. Blur's type of house?

5. Which band had a one-hit wonder with 'Spaceman'?

6. Pulp wondered if we'd meet up in what year?

7. The year of the release of 'The Man Who' album by Travis?

8. The song that got The Verve into trouble with The Rolling Stones in 1997?

9. Alanis Morissette's first global hit album?

10. Joan Osborne asked this question, "If God was --- -- --"?

2000s

1. Green Day wanted to be woken up when what ended?

2. Maroon 5's songs in 2002 were about who?

3. Snow Patrol were chasing what in 2006?

4. Elbow 2011 song 'Open ----'?

5. Florence and the Machine's 'You've Got the Love' appeared on which of their albums?

6. What type of shaped for Keane?

7. Kasabian wanted to shoot who?

8. 'What I've Done' featured an apocalyptic video from which American band?

9. Who addressed the President in 2006?

10. The Black Eyed Peas biggest selling single in the first decade of the 2000s?

The Who

1. The Who were previously known as The High -------?

2. Who was the deaf, dumb and blind kid?

3. What was the name of the drummer who replaced Keith Moon?

4. The Who's first single?

5. Pete Townshend's brother has often worked on Who material. What's his name?

6. Which member of The Who famously wore a 'skeleton suit'?

7. Which live Beatles recording did members of The Who sing on?

8. Who played Uncle Ernie in the film of 'Tommy'?

9. 'Won't Get Fooled Again' was on which Who album?

10. What mode of transport was magic to the band?

Blondie

1. Blondie's comeback hit in 1999?

2. Which early Blondie song mistakenly resulted in the group being labelled as punk?

3. True or false? Chris Stein once presented a cable TV show?

4. English bassist Nigel?

5. Blondie were touched by what in 1978?

6. 'Heart of Glass' was a hit in which year?

7. The iconic New York club that Blondie appeared at early in their career?

8. Blondie's first hit record was in which country?

9. A Blondie tidal song?

10. A kind of energy and a Blondie song from 1980?

Led Zeppelin

1. Guest female vocalist on 'Led Zeppelin IV'?

2. Which rock legend said that the group would go down like a lead balloon, which consequently inspired the name?

3. Which group was Jimmy Page in that had Keith Relf as its lead singer?

4. Led Zeppelin's last concert with John Bonham was where and in what year?

5. What was Led Zeppelin's final studio album?

6. Greek hero's last stand on 'Presence'?

7. John Paul Jones played which instruments on 'Stairway to Heaven'?

8. Robert Plant's boy's name nickname?

9. The year that Led Zeppelin's first studio album, 'Led Zeppelin', came out?

10. Led Zeppelin's reggae song on 'Houses of the Holy'?

Oasis

1. The video for which song featured Liam Gallagher surrounded by wildlife?

2. Oasis stressed the importance of being what?

3. The penultimate UK no. 1 single for Oasis?

4. Nickname for former Oasis bassist Paul McGuigan?

5. 'Don't Look Back in Anger' was released in which year?

6. Which album featured the band's first UK top 10 single?

7. The first Oasis gig was in what city?

8. Which guitarist joined Oasis on stage at Knebworth in 1996 to perform 'I Am the Walrus'?

9. 'Wonderwall' came from which album?

10. Which Slade hit did Oasis cover?

Nirvana

1. The year Nirvana's first album, 'Bleach', was released?

2. Who did Dave Grohl replace on drums?

3. An unfortunately named early band of Kurt Cobain and Krist Novoselic?

4. Nirvana's first label?

5. The year Kurt Cobain was born?

6. First Nirvana single?

7. How many studio albums did Nirvana release?

8. 'Nevermind' topped the US albums chart in what month in 1992?

9. What was the last track on the original 'Bleach' album?

10. Who produced 'In Utero'?

Progressive Rock

1. King Crimson were in the court of who?

2. The first hit single for Genesis?

3. Which song saw Yes speak up for a certain cetacean?

4. Emerson, Lake & Palmer's Keith Emerson performed 'America' with which '60s group?

5. True or false? Black Sabbath guitarist Tony Iommi briefly played with Jethro Tull?

6. Who sang lead vocal on Hawkwind's 'Silver Machine'?

7. Who was the lead singer of Family?

8. A slight name change for this earthy band, which moved in a different direction in the 1970s?

9. A former Beatles engineer who had a project?

10. A very percussive name for this group?

The Doors

1. She was a 20th Century what?

2. What was over?

3. The name of The Doors fifth studio album?

4. Jim Morrison was born in what year?

5. Which blind singer famously covered 'Light My Fire'?

6. Which Doors album features circus entertainers on the cover?

7. Which session bassists played on 'Morrison Hotel'?

8. The apocalyptic 'The End' first featured on which Doors album?

9. People are what?

10. A Greek or Spanish caravan?

Trains, Boats and Planes

1. For The Monkees the last train was to where?

2. A massive hit for Rod Stewart in 1975?

3. This flight was for which Rory Gallagher band?

4. Instrumental on 'Magical Mystery Tour'?

5. For The Doors this ship was made of what?

6. Jefferson Airplane anthem about these types of ships?

7. Yardbirds train kept what?

8. Name of this Beach Boys sailing vessel?

9. 'Aeroplane' was the B-side of a debut single called 'Sunshine Day', but by which British group?

10. 'Train Round the Bend' was waiting for which very influential group?

The Velvet Underground

1. She was sweet?

2. Who were the band waiting for?

3. The Velvets Christmassy member?

4. A simple yellow image on the Velvets debut album?

5. Candy, Lisa, Stephanie what?

6. A notion that wasn't too clear?

7. Beginning to see what?

8. A lot quicker than walk, walk, walk?

9. Usually a work-free morning?'

10. These will linger on?

Legal

1. The Clash found out what?

2. 'Law Man' was sung by which American group that specialised in psychedelia?

3. For The Who it was a what type of matter?

4. Dylan's innocent boxer?

5. A condemned man in this Bee Gees classic had to what?

6. A Stones song that was a message to their fans after a drugs bust?

7. Sham 69 were keen for a what?

8. A John Lennon tribute to an imprisoned activist?

9. For Elton, Saturday night was what?

10. Mob hit for The Specials?

Buffalo Springfield

1. Looking back Buffalo Springfield album?

2. This woman was into what type of music?

3. They were expecting to what in 1967?

4. A Buffalo Springfield song Neil Young sang lead vocal on - 'Mr. ----'?

5. A bird of a certain colour?

6. An arrow that probably couldn't be fired?

7. A hot Buffalo Springfield song?

8. A question asked of an attractive young woman?

9. Bats can be found like this?

10. The year Buffalo Springfield split up?

Jefferson Airplane

1. They did it without pay?

2. Soap can create this?

3. The day before tomorrow?

4. A girl's name, vineyard?

5. Jefferson Airplane's female vocalist before Grace Slick?

6. A psychedelic song written by Grace Slick while she was with The Great Society

7. A crazy lady who believed all that she read?

8. An unusual number of heads?

9. This lover was?

10. Good at looking after sheep?

Eyes

1. Van Morrison favourite?

2. Who classic?

3. Coldplay song from their second album?

4. Dylan's lady who wasn't from the highlands?

5. The eye of Survivor's magnificent creature?

6. The Small Faces perceptive eye?

7. Tina Turner's Bond song?

8. A song by The Creation and a favourite cover of The Sex Pistols?

9. For The Eagles these eyes weren't truthful?

10. Primal Scream's Nazi girl?

Britpop

1. A stretchy group?

2. A trio that said it would be okay in 1995?

3. Blur's tribute to the BBC's 'Shipping Forecast'?

4. Louise Wener was the lead singer of which group?

5. The Verve's poetic song from 'Urban Hymns'?

6. Pulp were from which English city?

7. This group's music was used regularly on the British TV programme 'TFI Friday'?

8. The times of Oasis fame?

9. A fashionable name for this group?

10. Not light therapy for Echobelly?

Indie Bands

1. A group's name that is also the name of a famous English public school?

2. A young-sounding group with a following?

3. Not a fast dive?

4. They wanted a revolution?

5. Nothing was going to stop them?

6. Singers of a tribute to 'Saturn 5'?

7. 'Bug' was an album for which band?

8. A group on Sarah Records that's also the name of a sea creature?

9. They recorded a song about the two most famous British bands of the 1960s?

10. A Liverpool group whose name includes an abbreviation for a great American city?

Food and Drink

1. The Move's 1969 number one?

2. A Syd Barrett-penned song for Pink Floyd?

3. A type of sunrise for The Eagles?

4. How many more of what on Dylan's 'Desire' album?

5. A trip to the dentist's awaits if you eat this from The Beatles 'White Album'?

6. An early Stranglers fruity hit?

7. Life was what for 10cc?

8. A popular type of crisps and a psychedelic number from The Rutles?

9. An early Thin Lizzy song, earlier covered by The Seekers?

10. A herb in the wilderness sang about by The Byrds?

610 Questions

Answers

The Beatles

1. Pete Best 2. 1943 3. Cynthia 4. 'Norwegian Wood (This Bird Has Flown)' - which was also the first instance of a sitar being heard on a rock record. 5. Bolton, Derby, Ayr and Newport 6. Ringo, who was confined to bed by a burst appendix and pleurisy. 7. 'Abbey Road' 8. Pop art legend Peter Blake 9. 'Let It Be' 10. Eric Clapton

Rock Chicks

1. Love and hate 2. America 3. Slick 4. Blackhearts 5. Siouxsie Sioux 6. Stevie Nicks 7. Nico 8. P!nk 9. Janis Joplin 10. Gaye Advert

The Kinks

1. 'Sunny Afternoon' 2. 'Celluloid (Heroes)' 3. 'Autumn (Almanac)' 4. 'Waterloo Sunset' 5. 'Arthur' 6. 'Mr. Pleasant' 7. 'Village Green (Preservation Society)' 8. 1966 9. 'Shindig' in 1965 10. 'Dead End (Street)'

David Bowie

1. 'Space Oddity', in 1975 - 6 years after it had first been released. 2. David Jones, and then Davy Jones. He changed his name to avoid confusion with Davy Jones of The Monkees. 3. Former Beatle John Lennon 4. Berlin 5. Peter Frampton 6. Switzerland 7. Bowie and his brother Terry 8. One eye appeared

to change colour after being struck during a fight at Bowie's school by long time friend George Underwood. The spat, over a girl, left Bowie with what appeared to be one blue eye, with the uninjured eye still brown. Though it seems more a case of it being an illusion, because one pupil was bigger than the other. 9. George Underwood! 10. Elvis Presley. Both were born on January 8th.

Love

1. 'I'm Not in Love' 2. Hot 3. 'Modern Love' 4. 'Whole Lotta Love' 5. Somebody 6. All Around 7. This crazy little thing 8. Reign o'er me 9. Sir - 'To Sir with Love' 10. Oxygen

Punk/New Wave

1. The Clash 2. 'Strange Town' 3. Magazine's Howard Devoto 4. ITV 5. Blitzkrieg 6. Tony Wilson 7. Rat Scabies 8. Joy Division - 'She's Lost Control' 9. The Police 10. Elvis Costello - '(I Don't Want to Go to) Chelsea'

Pink Floyd

1. Emily 2. UFO 3. Eugene 4. Pompeii 5. Pig, sheep, dog 6. 'The Dark Side of the Moon' 7. Seamus 8. A cow 9. 'Vera (Vera Lynn)' 10. 'The Division Bell'

The Beach Boys

1. 1966 2. Carl Wilson 3. True 4. 'Surf City' in 1962 5. Mike Love 6. Goats 7. '(Help Me) Rhonda' 8. Carl Wilson 9. 'The Smile Sessions' 10. False

Places

1. Blackburn 2. David Bowie 3. Ohio 4. California 5. Belfast 6. New York 7. Alabama 8. Leeds 9. Vienna 10. Amsterdam

Colours

1.Yellow 2. Blue 3. Red 4. Purple 5. Grey 6. Black 7. Green 8. Gold 9. White 10. Brown

Animals

1. Horses 2. Dog 3. 'Dolphin (Smile)' 4. '(I Dig a) Pony' 5. Tiger 6. '(White) Rabbit' 7. Cats 8. '(Like a) Bat (Out of Hell)' 9. Fox 10. '(The) Porpoise (Song)'

Radiohead

1. 'Airbag' 2. The Pretenders 3. 'In Rainbows' in 2007 4. 1996 5. 'The Eraser' 6. False 7. 1989 8. A Talking Heads song 9. 2 10. '2 + 2 = 5'

Psychedelic

1. Layne 2. Eight 3. Surrealistic 4. Bob Dylan 5. A hole 6. In-A-Gadda-Da-Vida 7. Dantalian's Chariot 8. The Who - 'I Can See for Miles' 9. This is the end 10. Itchycoo

The Rolling Stones

1. Mick Taylor 2. Phillip 3. Muddy Waters 4. John Lennon 5. 1969 6. 1970s 7. 66 8. Delia Smith 9. Lennon and McCartney 10. The Kennedys

Singers

1. Steampacket 2. Band of Joy 3. Aaron 4. Declan MacManus 5. Joy Division's Ian Curtis 6. Jim Morrison 7. Ray Davies - 'Lola' 8. Sting 9. Paula Yates 10. John Lydon

Bassists

1. Jack Bruce of Cream 2. Sting 3. Wyman, with '(Si, Si) Je suis un Rock Star' 4. Andy Fraser 5. Glen Matlock 6. Roger Waters of Pink Floyd 7. Suzi Quatro, who had a hit with 'Can the Can'. 8. Led

Zeppelin's John Paul Jones 9. Paul Simonon of The Clash 10. Flea of The Red Hot Chilli Peppers

Drummers

1. John Lydon, Public Image Limited 2. Richard Starkey 3. Mo Tucker 4. Cozy Powell 5. Bev Bevan 6. Bonham, Led Zeppelin 7. Paul Burgess 8. John Densmore, The Doors 9. Former Nirvana drummer and now Foo Fighters frontman Dave Grohl. 10. Sex Pistols drummer Paul Cook

Guitarists

1. Carlos Santana 2. Captain Sensible 3. Brian Jones 4. McGuinn 5. Matt Bellamy 6. Slash, Guns N' Roses 7. Stuart Adamson 8. Mick Ronson 9. Robbie Krieger 10. Jack White, The White Stripes

Keyboardists

1. Reg Dwight 2. 'Get Back' 3. The Nice 4. Richard Wright 5. Ray Manzarek 6. Rik Wakeman 7. Gillian Gilbert 8. Leon Russell 9. Jools Holland 10. Iain Stewart

Neil Young

1. '(Rockin') in the Free World' 2. 'Harvest Moon' 3. 'Ohio' 4. 'Decade' 5. 'Hey Hey, My My (Into the Black)' 6. A hearse 7. Crazy Horse 8. 'After the Gold Rush' 9. 'Cortez' 10. Godfather of Grunge

Numbers

1. 2525 2. 40 3. 500 miles 4. 5 5. 69 6. 2000 7. 17 8. 96 9. 1984 10. 2-4-6-8

Jimi Hendrix

1. Marshall 2. Chas Chandler 3. Electric 4. Little Richard 5. Monterey 6. Seattle 7. True, he broke his ankle while on duty. 8. Band of Gypsies 9. 'Purple

Haze' 10. Cherokee

Heavy Rock

1. 'Hush' 2. Iron Maiden 3. 'Smoke (on the Water)' 4. Tony Iommi of Black Sabbath 5. Rainbow 6. 1969 7. Painted Lady 8. Saxon 9. Ian Fraser Kilmister 10. Whitesnake

The Sex Pistols

1. 'Green' 2. 'EMI' 3. Pink Floyd (though Johnny actually likes them) 4. 'So It Goes' - a few weeks before their Bill Grundy interview. 5. Sex 6. Steve Jones 7. John Ritchie 8. 'Something Else' 9. 1975 10. Winterland, San Francisco

Sun and Moon

1. 'Set the Controls for the Heart of the Sun' 2. 'Here Comes the Sun' 3. 'Ice in the Sun' 4. 'Holidays in the Sun' 5. 'Man on the Moon' 6. 'Bad Moon Rising' 7. 'The Sun Ain't Gonna Shine (Anymore)' 8. 'TV' 9. 'Blue Moon' 10. 'The Killing Moon'

Bob Dylan

1. 'The Freewheelin' Bob Dylan', which was released in 1963. 2. Robert Zimmerman 3. 'Desire' 4. 'Mr. Tambourine Man' in 1965 5. 'Don't Look Back' 6. 'Maggie's Farm' 7. 1965 8. 'She Loves You', with Dylan thinking the line "I can't hide" was "We get high". 9. David Bowie, with 'Song For Bob Dylan', which appeared on 'Hunky Dory'. 10. George Harrison, on his 1971 album, 'All Things Must Pass'.

U2

1. 1987 2. Jack Nicholson 3. 'Stuck in a Moment You Can't Get Out Of' 4. Paul Hewson (Bono), Dave Evans (The Edge) 5. 'October' 6. 'Achtung

Baby' 7. 'The Unforgettable Fire' 8. 'Sgt. Pepper's Lonely Hearts Club Band' 9. Paul Whitehouse 10. Adam Clayton

Girls and Boys

1. 'Alison' 2. 'Daniel' 3. 'Eloise' 4. 'Valerie' 5. 'Christine' 6. Robert 7. 'Gloria' 8. Gordon 9. 'Debora' 10. Mary

The Byrds

1. Easy Rider 2. You 3. 'Mr. Tambourine Man' 4. John 5. Mare 6. Byrd 7. 'Turn! Turn! Turn!' 8. Alright 9. 5th 10. Time

Fleetwood Mac

1. Hartlepool 2. 1968 3. Christine McVie 4. John Mayall & The Bluesbreakers. 5.'Tusk' in 1979 6. 1975 7. Bassist Bob Brunning and Jeremy Spencer. Peter Green had named the group after Mick Fleetwood and John McVie, hoping that McVie would join the newly formed band immediately, though he did a few weeks later. 8. The 1975 album, 'Fleetwood Mac'. 9. Danny Kirwan 10. 'Man of the World'

Bruce Springsteen

1. Patti Smith 2. The East Street Band 3. 1975 4. The Gaslight Anthem 5. 'Philadelphia' - 'Streets Of Philadelphia' 6. Manfred Mann's Earth Band 7. Bob Dylan 8. 'Born in the U.S.A.' 9. 1973 ('Greetings from Asbury Park, N.J.') 10. 'Girls in Their Summer Clothes'

Eric Clapton

1. John Mayall & The Bluesbreakers 2. 'Eric Clapton Is God' 3. March 30th, 1945. 4. 'Layla' 5. 1965 6. Blind Faith 7. The Royal Albert Hall 8. Bob

Marley 9. 'Wonderful Tonight' 10. George Harrison

The Moody Blues

1. Leary 2. 'Go Now' 3. 'Days of Future Passed' 4. Graeme Edge 5. Birmingham 6. 1964 7. ('In Search of) the Lost Chord' 8. Denny Laine 9. Mike Pinder 10. 'A Question of Balance'

Days and Nights

1. 'Nights in White Satin' 2. 'A Hard Day's Night' 3. 'Days' 4. 'I Drove All Night' 5. 'Tonight's the Night (Gonna Be Alright)' 6. 'These Are the Days of Our Lives' 7. 'It's a Beautiful Day Today' 8. 'Whatever Gets You Thru the Night' 9. 'Have a Nice Day' 10. 'Let's Spend the Night Together'

Queen

1. 1974 2. 'Death on Two Legs (Dedicated to...)' 3. 'I Want to Break Free' 4. Roger Taylor's son saying 'Radio CaCa'. 5. Smile, which featured Brian May, Roger Taylor and latterly Freddie Mercury. 6. 'You're My Best Friend' 7. 'News of the World' 8. 'Crazy Little Thing Called Love' in 1980. 9. 'Flash Gordon' 10. Budapest

Elton John

1. Fantastic 2. 'Your Song' in 1970 3. 1976 4. 'Get It On' 5. Standing 6. Marilyn Monroe 7. Blues 8. 'Crocodile Rock' 9. Watford 10. DJM Records (Dick James Music)

Rod Stewart

1. 'In a Broken Dream', for which Rod was allegedly paid for his services with car seat covers! 2. 'Maggie May' in 1971. 3. 'Atlantic Crossing' 4. The Jeff Beck Group, which also included future Faces guitarist Ronnie Wood. 5. 1977 6. 'The First

Cut Is the Deepest/I Don't Want to Talk About It' 7. Brentford 8. 'Incidentally' 9. ('Reason to) Believe' 10. 'The Great American Songbook'

Coldplay

1. 'Parachutes' 2. 1977 3. 2000 4. Eight 5. London 6. The Laurel Tree, Camden, London. 7. 2002 8. 'A Rush of Blood to the Head' 9. 'Buffy the Vampire Slayer' 10. 'Charlie Brown'

Weather

1. 'Hurricane' 2. 'Rain' - the first pop song to feature a backwards guitar. 3. 'Sunny' 4. 'Why Does It Always Rain on Me?' 5. 'Riders on the Storm' 6. 'Red Rain' 7. 'What Have They Done to the Rain' 8. 'Catch the Wind' 9. 'Sunshine of Your Love' 10. 'Blowin' in the Wind'

The Police

1. Stewart Copeland 2. True 3. 1983 4. 'Every Breath You Take' 5. 'Synchronicity' 6. Gordon Sumner 7. 'Roxanne' 8. Stewart Copeland 9. Ace Face 10. Illegal Records

1960s

1. Thunderclap Newman 2. Tennis 3. Tony Iommi 4. Honey Lantree 5. Alan Clarke 6. Penny 7. Canterbury 8. Conspiracy 9. A fan of The Grateful Dead. 10. Canned Heat

1970s

1. 'I'm Mandy Fly Me' 2. 'Spiral Scratch' 3. 1976 4. 'Songbird' 5. 'Metal (Guru)' 6. '(The) Model'. Recorded in 1978 this song topped the UK singles chart in 1982. 7. 'Ballroom (Blitz)' 8. 'No Fun' 9. Humble Pie 10. '(Cum On Feel the) Noize'

1980s

1. '(Against All) Odds (Take a Look at Me Now)' 2. 'Come On Eileen' 3. Diana Dors 4. 'Time After Time' 5. Stupid 6. 'Meat Is Murder' 7. 'Joan of Arc' and 'Maid of Orleans'. 8. 'I Got You Babe' 9. '(I Want to Know) What Love Is' 10. 'Rapture' in 1980.

1990s

1. 'The Great Beyond' 2. 'Live Forever' 3. '(Just) Looking' 4. 'Country (House)' 5. Babylon Zoo 6. '2000 (Disco 2000)' 7. 1999 8. 'Bittersweet Symphony' 9. 'Little Jagged Pill' 10. 'One of Us'

2000s

1. '(Wake Me Up When) September (Ends)' 2. '(Songs About) Jane' 3. '(Chasing) Cars' 4. 'Arms' 5. 'Lungs' 6. 'Bedshaped' 7. '(Shoot) the Runner' 8. Linkin Park 9. P!nk - 'Dear Mr. President' 10. 'I Gotta Feeling' in 2009.

The Who

1. Numbers 2. Tommy 3. Kenney Jones 4. 'I Can't Explain' 5. Simon Townshend 6. John Entwistle 7. 'All You Need Is Love' 8. Keith Moon 9. 'Who's Next' 10. '(Magic) Bus'

Blondie

1. 'Maria' 2. 'Rip Her to Shreds' 3. True 4. Nigel Harrison 5. '(I'm Always) Touched (by Your Presence, Dear)' 6. 1979 7. CBGBs 8. Australia - 'In the Flesh', which reached no. 2. 9. 'The Tide Is High' 10. 'Atomic'

Led Zeppelin

1. Sandy Denny 2. Keith Moon 3. The Yardbirds 4. Berlin in 1980. 5. 'In Through the Out Door' 6.

Achilles 7. Mandolin, harp, organ. 8. Percy 9. 1969 10. 'D'yer Mak'er'

Oasis

1. 'I'm Outta Time' 2. '(The Importance of Being) Idle' 3. 'Lyla' 4. Guigsy 5. 1996 6. 'Live Forever' on 'Definitely Maybe'. 7. Manchester 8. Stone Roses guitarist John Squire. 9. '(What's the Story) Morning Glory?' 10. 'Cum On Feel the Noize'

Nirvana

1. 1989 2. Chad Channing 3. Stiff Woodies 4. Sub Pop 5. 1967 6. 'Love Buzz' in 1988. 7. Just three - 'Bleach' in 1989, 'Nevermind' in 1991, and 'In Utero' in 1993. 8. January 9. 'Sifting' 10. Steve Albini

Progressive Rock

1. '(In the Court of) the Crimson King' 2. 'I Know What I Like (In Your Wardrobe)' 3. 'Don't Kill the Whale' 4. The Nice 5. True 6. Lemmy 7. Roger Chapman 8. Manfred Mann's Earth Band 9. (The) Alan Parsons (Project) 10. Gong

The Doors

1. '(20th Century) Fox' 2. '(When the) Music ('s Over)' 3. 'Morrison Hotel' 4. 1943 5. José Feliciano 6. 'Strange Days' 7. Lonnie Mack and Ray Neapolitan. 8. The eponymous 'The Doors' - their debut album. 9. '(People Are) Strange' 10. 'Spanish (Caravan)'

Trains, Boats and Planes

1. Clarksville 2. 'Sailing' 3. Nazareth - 'This Flight Tonight' 4. 'Flying' 5. Crystal 6. Wooden 7. Rollin' ('Train Kept a Rollin'') 8. 'Sloop John B' 9. Jethro Tull, though mistakenly credited at the time as Jethro Toe. 10. The Velvet Underground

The Velvet Underground

1. Jane 2. ('I'm Waiting for') The Man 3. Doug Yule 4. Banana 5. Says 6. Foggy 7. The Light 8. 'Run Run Run' 9. Sunday 10. 'Pale Blue Eyes'

Legal

1. ('I Fought the Law') and the law won 2. Jefferson Airplane 3. 'A Legal Matter' 4. 'Hurricane' 5. '('I've Gotta) Get a Message to You' 6. 'We Love You' 7. A 'Borstal Breakout' 8. 'John Sinclair' 9. '(Saturday Night's) Alright for Fighting' 10. 'Gangsters'

Buffalo Springfield

1. 'Retrospective' 2. 'Rock and Roll' 3. Fly 4. Soul 5. 'Bluebird' 6. 'Broken Arrow' 7. 'Burned' 8. 'Pretty Girl Why' 9. 'Hung Upside Down' 10. 1968 (though they reformed with Neil Young, Stephen Stills and Richie Furay for some concerts in 2010)

Jefferson Airplane

1. 'Volunteers' 2. 'Lather' 3. 'Today' 4. 'Martha' 5. Signe Toly Anderson 6. 'White Rabbit' 7. 'Crazy Miranda' 8. 'Two Heads' 9. 'Plastic Fantastic (Lover)' 10. 'Good Shepherd'

Eyes

1. 'Brown Eyed Girl' 2. 'Behind Blue Eyes' 3. 'Green Eyes' 4. 'Sad-Eyed Lady of the Lowlands' 5. 'Eye of the Tiger' 6. 'My Mind's Eye' 7. 'GoldenEye' 8. 'Through My Eyes' 9. 'Lyin' Eyes' 10. 'Swastika Eyes'

Britpop

1. Elastica 2. Supergrass with 'Alright'. 3. 'This Is a Low' 4. Sleeper 5. 'Sonnet' 6. Sheffield 7. Ocean Colour Scene 8. 'The Hindu Times' 9. Menswear 10.

'Dark Therapy'

Indie Bands

1. Chapterhouse 2. Teenage Fanclub 3. Slowdive 4. Spacemen 3 5. Saint Etienne - 'Nothing Can Stop Us' 6. Inspiral Carpets 7. Dinosaur Jr. 8. The Sea Urchins 9. The House of Love - 'Beatles and the Stones' 10. The La's

Food and Drink

1. 'Blackberry Way' 2. 'Apples and Oranges' 3. 'Tequila Sunrise' 4. 'One More Cup of Coffee' 5. 'Savoy Truffle' 6. 'Peaches' 7. ('Life Is) a Minestrone' 8. 'Cheese and Onions' 9. 'Whiskey in the Jar' 10. 'Wild Mountain Thyme'

610 Questions

500 or more correct answers – you probably are a rock nerd

400-500 correct answers – impressive rock knowledge

300-400 correct answers
– pretty good

200-300 correct answers
– a worthy effort

100-200 correct answers
– you need to listen to more rock, and read more rock-related articles

Under 100 correct answers
– maybe folk, hip hop or soul will be more your thing

Rock Mathematics

Add the following together to come up with a specific year.

1. The number of letters in the surname of the leader of the band Love?

2. The year The Beatles first single was released?

3. The number of Clarks and Clarkes in the early line-up of The Byrds?

4. Number of years Keith Moon was in The Who?

5. The amount of number one singles Bob Dylan has had in the UK?

Rock Alphabet

A 'How Long' was a '70s hit for them?

B Ginger Baker's army?

C The goth band whose name suggested a devout following?

D A gentle bird name for this group?

E Hot Rods Christian name?

F Nonsensical PiL track from their first album?

G 'The Brazilian' instrumental was by this legendary British group?

H A Neanderthal hit for them?

I A famous Ian McNabb group of the 1980s?

J Judy was their girl, and she wore a certain disguise?

K They sang about 'My Sharona'?

L Kasabian's home city?

M They sang about 'Pop Muzik' in 1979?

N A band name that Jesus would have identified with?

O Marmalade cover of a Beatles song?

P Russian girls with attitude?

Q Kinks bassist?

R Mr. Stewart's (full) Christian name?

S A cutting guitarist who has a liking for top hats?

T Rory Gallagher's band appealed to one of the senses?

U Early U2 album?

V '70s song about a troubled Dutch painter?

W They were 'Blowin' Free' in the 1970s?

X A magical land for Dave Dee, Dozy, Beaky, Mick & Tich?

Y They wanted to 'Get Together'?

Z The man with the big moustache and the inventive band?

Rock Geography

1. Aphrodite's Child were a band from which European country?

2. 'Radar Love' was a 1973 hit for Golden Earring, but which country did they come from?

3. Men at Work were from Australia or New Zealand?

4. 'Turning Japanese' was a 1980 hit for whom?

5. David Bowie's girl was from where in 1983?

6. 'Take My Breath Away' in this German city?

7. The legendary 1969 Woodstock festival was held in which American state?

8. Plastic Bertrand hails from this country?

9. PiL live album from 1980 was recorded in this city?

10. Early name for Joy Division?

Rock Biology

1. Big Brother and the Holding Company 1968 hit?

2. A point of the arm from Bury, Greater Manchester?

3. Big cat feet 1974 hit?

4. Pretty Things song, but normally worn on the arm?

5. This was silent for New Order in 1983?

6. They didn't lie for Shakira in 2006?

7. Scary, and the rest may have fallen out for this band?

8. A slight movement by Queen in 1974?

9. Stones 1965 album?

10. Skunk Anansie singer?

Answers

Rock Mathematics

1981

1. 3 (Arthur Lee) 2. 1962 3. 2 (Gene Clark and Michael Clarke) 4. 14 (1964-1978) 5. 0

Rock Alphabet

A. Ace. B. Baker Gurvitz Army C. The Cult D. Doves E. Eddie (Eddie and the Hot Rods) F. 'Fodderstompf' G. Genesis H Hotlegs ('Neanderthal Man') I. The Icicle Works J. John Fred & His Playboy Band ('Judy in Disguise (With Glasses)') K. The Knack L. Leicester M. M N. Nazareth O. 'Ob-La-Di, Ob-La-Da' P. Pussy Riot Q. Pete Quaife R. Roderick S. Slash T. Taste U. 'Under a Blood Red Sky' V. 'Vincent' by Don McLean. W. Wishbone Ash X. ('The Legend of) Xanadu' Y. The Youngbloods Z. Frank Zappa and The Mothers of Invention

Rock Geography

1. Greece 2. The Netherlands 3. Australia 4. The Vapors 5. 'China (Girl)' 6. Berlin 7. New York 8. Belgium 9. Paris 10. Warsaw

Rock Biology

1. 'Piece of My Heart' 2. Elbow 3. 'Tiger Feet' by Mud. 4. 'Bracelets of Fingers' 5. 'Your Silent Face'

6. 'Hips Don't Lie' 7. Spooky Tooth 8. 'Flick of the Wrist' 9. 'Out of Our Heads' 10. Skin

References

Personal knowledge

https://www.nme.com/

Wikipedia

The Guardian website

https://www.u2.com/

https://www.thewho.com/

https://www.songmeaningsandfacts.com/

YouTube

About the Author

Paul Rance was born in Luton in 1959 and grew up in the Warden Hill and Leagrave areas of the town. Beginning as a poet in the early 1980s, Paul moved to the Lincolnshire village of Whaplode Drove in 1983. There he founded small publishing company Peace & Freedom Press in 1985, and the website, booksmusicfilmstv.com, in 2005. Paul was part of the underground rock group The Peace & Freedom Band, who were one of the first British groups to record an album in mp3 format in 2000, through American company, mp3.com. Paul now concentrates more on writing and art, and, though no one believes him (!), James Bond music composer David Arnold was a one-time neighbour and friend.

Paul Rance books on Amazon.co.uk
http://www.amazon.co.uk/Paul-Rance/e/B004P2ALYY/ref=ntt_athr_dp_pel_pop_1

Paul Rance books on Amazon.com
http://www.amazon.com/author/paulrance

Paul Rance's website
https://www.paulrance.com

Paul Rance books available from Amazon in paperback and Kindle format.

Paul Rance's Nonsense Creatures: Limericks and Illustrations
Paul Rance rediscovered Edward Lear in 2009, and began creating his own nonsense creatures - in the form of illustrations and limericks. Originally published on Associated Content in 2009, here are the first batch of limericks, which should appeal to children aged 3 to 120.

50 Great Moments and Memories of the 1960s
From a British perspective, here's a look back at some of the greatest moments and people from the 1960s, including The Beatles, First Man on the Moon, Woodstock, Bob Dylan, Muhammad Ali, Twiggy, David Bailey, England winning the World Cup, The Rolling Stones, Martin Luther King, James Bond, *Doctor Who* and *Star Trek*.

Music pages of interest...
THE PEACE & FREEDOM BAND

The Peace & Freedom Band on ReverbNation
https://www.reverbnation.com/thepeacefreedomband

FULL MOON POET

Search for **FullMoonMusic** here
https://www.amazon.co.uk/

STEVE ANDREWS

A review of Steve's most recent album, *Songs Of The Now And Then*, by Paul Rance that appeared in the Spring 2020 issue of *Peace & Freedom* magazine.

Nature lovers, rebels everywhere, listen up! Steve Andrews offers some luscious sounds and thought-provoking lyrics on songs such as plastic pollution (*Where Does All The Plastic Go?*), *The Nightingale* and *Citizen Of Earth*. The gorgeously rich sound of *Harvest Home* sets the tone of the album, while the uptempo *Butterfly In My Beard* is an autobiographical song.

Steve is ably supported by multi-instrumentalist

Jayce Lewis (who also produced, engineered and mixed this album), and Mab Jones on backing vocals.

Songs Of The Now And Then album available from bandcamp
https://bardofely.bandcamp.com/album/songs-of-the-now-and-then

Wide range of Steve's songs on ReverbNation
https://www.reverbnation.com/bardofely/songs

✱✱✱✱✱✱✱✱

EXILE POTS

An eponymous album of 56 instrumental tracks gathered from EP's work from 1993 to 2017, including 23 exclusive tracks. A wide range of sounds and moods here.

Available from bandcamp
https://exilepots.bandcamp.com/album/exile-pots

✺✺✺✺✺✺✺✺

On the front of The Red Lion Hotel, Spalding, Lincolnshire. Photograph by Paul Rance.

Printed in Great Britain
by Amazon